THE RULE OF THE THEOTOKOS ACCORDING TO SAINT SERAPHIM OF SAROV

ILLUSTRATED WITH ICONS AND RELICS

Hope and Life Press

First published in 2017 by
HOPE AND LIFE PRESS

The Rule of the Theotokos According to Saint Seraphim of Sarov

ISBN 978-0-9990447-3-5

Copyright © 2017 Hope and Life Press – All rights reserved.
The front cover shows the Kursk-Root icon of the Theotokos.

Published by
HOPE AND LIFE PRESS
2312 Chemin Herron #A, Dorval QC, H9S 1C5 Canada; and
P.O. Box 37, East Longmeadow, MA 01028, USA.
http://hopeandlifepress.com
hopeandlifepress@gmail.com

All rights reserved. No part of this work may be reproduced, stored in a retrieval system, or submitted in any form or by any means, electronic, mechanical, photocopying, recording or otherwise, without the prior written permission of the publisher. This book may not be lent, resold, hired out or otherwise disposed of by way of trade in any form of binding or cover other than that in which it is published, without the prior written consent of the published.

Printed in the United States of America.

Between all the various parts of the Church there is a bond of close communion whereby spiritual riches...are shared. For the members of the People of God are called upon to share their goods (as in the words of the apostle), 'according to the gift that each has received administer it to one another as good stewards of the manifold grace of God (1 Pet 5:10).

~ *Lumen Gentium* §13 ~

CONTENTS

Introduction	7
THE RULE OF THE THEOTOKOS ACCORDING TO SAINT SERAPHIM OF SAROV	9
1. First Decade – The Birth of the Theotokos	13
2. Second Decade – The Presentation of the Theotokos	15
3. Third Decade – The Annunciation of the Lord's Birth	17
4. Fourth Decade – The Meeting of the Theotokos and Saint Elizabeth	19
5. Fifth Decade – The Birth of the Lord	21
6. Sixth Decade – The Prophecy of Saint Symeon	23
7. Seventh Decade – The Flight into Egypt	25
8. Eighth Decade – The Boy-Christ Among the Doctors	27
9. Ninth Decade – The Wedding at Cana	29
10. Tenth Decade – The Crucifixion of the Lord	31
11. Eleventh Decade – The Resurrection of the Lord	33
12. Twelfth Decade – The Ascension of the Lord into Heaven	35
13. Thirteenth Decade – Pentecost	37
14. Fourteenth Decade – Dormition of the Theotokos	39
15. Fifthteenth Decade – Crowning of the Theotokos by the Holy Trinity	41
Relics of the Theotokos	43
List of Icons	47
List of Relics	48
Select Hope and Life Press Books	49

Saint Seraphim of Sarov

INTRODUCTION

In this book you will find the prayer rule that the Virgin Mary, the Mother of God, had given to a monk in the Thebaid of Egypt in the early eighth century. It was later revived by Saint Seraphim of Sarov, who advocated that his spiritual children say it every day. Among these was the Hieromartyr Seraphim Zevzdinsky, who added the prayer *Open unto us the door of your loving kindness*. According to the writings of another spiritual son, Father Zosima, all Christians used to pray this rule:

> *I forgot to give you a piece of advice vital for salvation. Say the O Hail, Mother of God and Virgin one hundred and fifty times, and this prayer will lead you on the way to salvation. This rule was given by the Mother of God herself in about the eighth century and at one time all Christians fulfilled it.*

The prayer rule is also known to be practised every day on Mount Athos.

The Rule of the Theotokos comprises introductory and final prayers, 150 recitations of the Angelic Salutation with 15 meditations as follows and accompanying prayers:

1. The Birth of the Theotokos
2. The Presentation of the Theotokos
3. The Annunciation of the Lord's Birth
4. The Meeting of the Theotokos and Saint Elizabeth
5. The Birth of the Lord
6. The Prophecy of Saint Simeon
7. The Flight into Egypt
8. The Boy-Christ Among the Doctors

9. The Wedding at Cana
10. The Crucifixion of the Lord
11. The Resurrection of the Lord
12. The Ascension of the Lord into Heaven
13. Pentecost
14. The Dormition of the Theotokos
15. The Crowning of the Theotokos by the Holy Trinity.

The introductory prayers are derived from the revealed Rule of Saint Pachomius.[1] Each meditation is accompanied by its relevant traditional icon in full color to facilitate prayer. Also presented are photographs of some relics of the Theotokos for the meditative edification of the reader.

---

[1] According to tradition, this little rule was given to Saint Pachomius by an angel.

THE RULE OF THE THEOTOKOS

According to
Saint Seraphim of Sarov

Sign of the Cross: In the Name of the Father, the Son, and the Holy Spirit. Amen.

Introductory Prayers

God be merciful to me, a sinner. Glory to You, our God, glory to You.

O Heavenly King, Comforter, Spirit of Truth, Who are everywhere present and fills all things, O Treasury of every good and Bestower of life: come and dwell in us, and cleanse us from every stain, and save our souls, O Good One.

Holy God, Holy Mighty One, Holy Immortal One, have mercy on us (*Three times*).

Glory to the Father, and to the Son, and to the Holy Spirit, both now and ever and unto the ages of ages. Amen.

O Most Holy Trinity, have mercy on us. O Lord, blot out our sins. O Master, pardon our iniquities. O Holy One, visit and heal our infirmities, for Your Name's sake.

Lord, have mercy (*Three times*).

Glory to the Father, and to the Son, and to the Holy Spirit, both now and ever and unto the ages of ages. Amen.

The "Our Father:" Our Father, Who are in heaven, hallowed be Your Name. Your kingdom come, Your will be done on earth as it is in heaven. Give us this day our daily bread and forgive us our trespasses as we forgive those who trespass against us. And lead us not into temptation, but deliver us from the Evil One.

Lord, have mercy (*Three times*).

Glory to the Father, and to the Son, and to the Holy Spirit, both now and ever and unto the ages of ages. Amen.

O come let us worship God our King. O come, let us worship and fall down before Christ our King and God. O come, let us worship and fall down before Christ Himself, our King and God.

The Creed: I believe in one God, the Father Almighty, Creator of heaven and earth, and of all things visible and invisible. I believe in one Lord, Jesus Christ, the only-begotten Son of God, begotten of the Father before all ages; Light of Light, true God of true God, begotten, not created, of one essence with the Father, through Whom all things were made. Who for us men and for our salvation came down from heaven and was incarnate of the Holy Spirit and the Virgin Mary and became man. He was crucified for us under Pontius Pilate and suffered and was buried.

And He rose on the third day, according to the Scriptures. He ascended into heaven and is seated at the right hand of the Father, from where He will come again with glory to judge the living and dead. His kingdom shall have no end. I believe in the Holy Spirit, the Lord, the Creator of life, Who proceeds from the Father, Who together with the Father and the Son is worshipped and glorified, Who spoke through the prophets. In one, holy, catholic and apostolic Church, I confess one baptism for the forgiveness of sins. I look for the resurrection of the dead and the life of the age to come. Amen.

O Lord, open my lips and my mouth shall proclaim Your praise.

The Birth of the Theotokos

First Decade

The Birth of the Theotokos

Let us remember the birth of the Mother of God. Let us pray for mothers, fathers and children.

Rejoice, O Virgin, Mother of God, Mary, full of grace, the Lord is with you. Blessed are you among women and blessed is the fruit of your womb, for you have borne the Savior of our souls (Ten times).

After: Our Lady, Blessed Mother of God, save and preserve your servants (names of parents, relatives, friends), increase their faith and repentance, and when they die give them rest with the saints in your eternal glory.

Our Father, Who are in heaven, hallowed be Your Name. Your kingdom come, Your will be done on earth as it is in heaven. Give us this day our daily bread and forgive us our trespasses as we forgive those who trespass against us. And lead us not into temptation, but deliver us from the Evil One.

Open unto us the door of your loving kindness, O most blessed Mother of God. As we set our hope in you, let us not be confounded, but through you may we be delivered from all adversities. For you are the salvation of the Christian race.

The Entrance of the Theotokos in the Temple

Second Decade

The Presentation of the Theotokos

Let us remember the feast of the Presentation of the Blessed Virgin and Mother of God. Let us pray for those who have lost their way and fallen away from the Church.

Rejoice, O Virgin, Mother of God, Mary, full of grace, the Lord is with you. Blessed are you among women and blessed is the fruit of your womb, for you have borne the Savior of our souls (Ten times).

After: Our Lady, Blessed Mother of God, save and preserve and unite or reunite to the Holy Church your servants who have lost their path and fallen away (names).

Our Father, Who are in heaven, hallowed be Your Name. Your kingdom come, Your will be done on earth as it is in heaven. Give us this day our daily bread and forgive us our trespasses as we forgive those who trespass against us. And lead us not into temptation, but deliver us from the Evil One.

Open unto us the door of your loving kindness, O most blessed Mother of God. As we set our hope in you, let us not be confounded, but through you may we be delivered from all adversities. For you are the salvation of the Christian race.

The Annunciation of the Lord's Birth by the Archangel Gabriel

Third Decade

The Annunciation of the Lord's Birth

Let us remember the Annunciation of the Blessed Mother of God. Let us pray for the soothing of sorrows and the consolation of those who grieve.

Rejoice, O Virgin, Mother of God, Mary, full of grace, the Lord is with you. Blessed are you among women and blessed is the fruit of your womb, for you have borne the Savior of our souls (Ten times).

After: Our Lady, Blessed Mother of God, soothe our sorrows and send consolation to your servants who are grieving and ill (names).

Our Father, Who are in heaven, hallowed be Your Name. Your kingdom come, Your will be done on earth as it is in heaven. Give us this day our daily bread and forgive us our trespasses as we forgive those who trespass against us. And lead us not into temptation, but deliver us from the Evil One.

Open unto us the door of your loving kindness, O most blessed Mother of God. As we set our hope in you, let us not be confounded, but through you may we be delivered from all adversities. For you are the salvation of the Christian race.

The Visitation of the Theotokos with Righteous Elizabeth

Fourth Decade

The Meeting of the Theotokos and Saint Elizabeth

Let us remember the meeting of the Blessed Virgin with the righteous Elizabeth. Let us pray for the reunion of the separated, for those whose dear ones or children are living away from them or missing.

Rejoice, O Virgin, Mother of God, Mary, full of grace, the Lord is with you. Blessed are you among women and blessed is the fruit of your womb, for you have borne the Savior of our souls (Ten times).

After: Our Lady, Blessed Mother of God, unite your servants who are separated.

Our Father, Who are in heaven, hallowed be Your Name. Your kingdom come, Your will be done on earth as it is in heaven. Give us this day our daily bread and forgive us our trespasses as we forgive those who trespass against us. And lead us not into temptation, but deliver us from the Evil One.

Open unto us the door of your loving kindness, O most blessed Mother of God. As we set our hope in you, let us not be confounded, but through you may we be delivered from all adversities. For you are the salvation of the Christian race.

The Nativity of the Lord, Jesus Christ

Fifth Decade

The Birth of the Lord

Let us remember the Birth of Christ. Let us pray for the rebirth of souls, for new life in Christ.

Rejoice, O Virgin, Mother of God, Mary, full of grace, the Lord is with you. Blessed are you among women and blessed is the fruit of your womb, for you have borne the Savior of our souls (Ten times).

After: Our Lady, Blessed Mother of God, grant unto me, who has been baptized in Christ, to be clothed in Christ.

Our Father, Who are in heaven, hallowed be Your Name. Your kingdom come, Your will be done on earth as it is in heaven. Give us this day our daily bread and forgive us our trespasses as we forgive those who trespass against us. And lead us not into temptation, but deliver us from the Evil One.

Open unto us the door of your loving kindness, O most blessed Mother of God. As we set our hope in you, let us not be confounded, but through you may we be delivered from all adversities. For you are the salvation of the Christian race.

The Presentation of the Lord in the Temple

Sixth Decade

The Prophecy of Saint Simeon

Let us remember the Feast of the Purification of the Lord and the words uttered by Saint Simeon: *Yes, a sword shall also pierce through your own soul.* Let us pray that the Mother of God will meet our souls at the hour of our death and will contrive that we receive the Holy Sacrament with our last breath, and will lead our souls through the terrible torments.

Rejoice, O Virgin, Mother of God, Mary, full of grace, the Lord is with you. Blessed are you among women and blessed is the fruit of your womb, for you have borne the Savior of our souls (Ten times).

After: Our Lady, Blessed Mother of God, let me receive the Holy Sacrament with my last breath, and lead my soul yourself through the terrible torments.

Our Father, Who are in heaven, hallowed be Your Name. Your kingdom come, Your will be done on earth as it is in heaven. Give us this day our daily bread and forgive us our trespasses as we forgive those who trespass against us. And lead us not into temptation, but deliver us from the Evil One.

Open unto us the door of your loving kindness, O most blessed Mother of God. As we set our hope in you, let us not be confounded, but through you may we be delivered from all adversities. For you are the salvation of the Christian race.

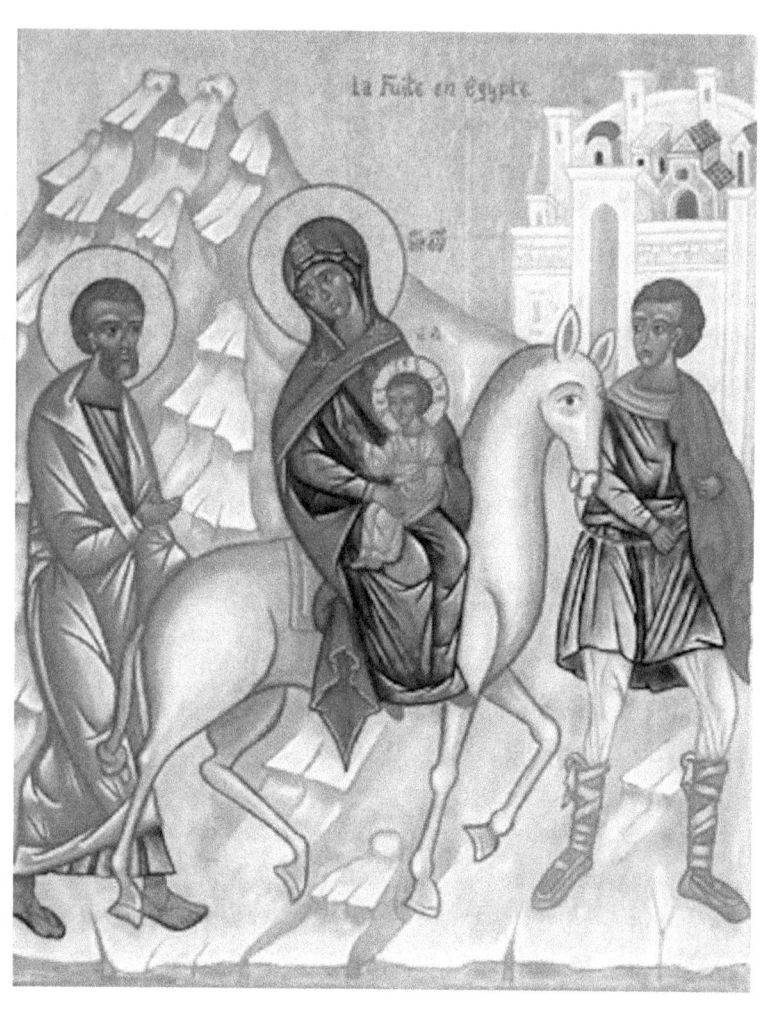

The Flight into Egypt

Seventh Decade

The Flight into Egypt

Let us remember the flight of the Mother of God with the God-Child into Egypt. Let us pray that the Mother of God will help us avoid temptation in this life and deliver us from misfortunes.

Rejoice, O Virgin, Mother of God, Mary, full of grace, the Lord is with you. Blessed are you among women and blessed is the fruit of your womb, for you have borne the Savior of our souls (Ten times).

After: Our Lady, Blessed Mother of God, help me avoid temptation in this life and deliver me from misfortunes.

Our Father, Who are in heaven, hallowed be Your Name. Your kingdom come, Your will be done on earth as it is in heaven. Give us this day our daily bread and forgive us our trespasses as we forgive those who trespass against us. And lead us not into temptation, but deliver us from the Evil One.

Open unto us the door of your loving kindness, O most blessed Mother of God. As we set our hope in you, let us not be confounded, but through you may we be delivered from all adversities. For you are the salvation of the Christian race.

The Young Christ Teaching the Doctors in the Temple

Eighth Decade

The Boy-Christ Among the Doctors

Let us remember the disappearance of the twelve-year-old Boy, Jesus, in Jerusalem and the sorrow of the Mother of God on this account. Let us pray, begging the Mother of God for the constant repetition of the Jesus Prayer.[2]

Rejoice, O Virgin, Mother of God, Mary, full of grace, the Lord is with you. Blessed are you among women and blessed is the fruit of your womb, for you have borne the Savior of our souls (Ten times).

After: Our Lady, Blessed Mother of God, grant to me the unceasing Jesus Prayer.

Our Father, Who are in heaven, hallowed be Your Name. Your kingdom come, Your will be done on earth as it is in heaven. Give us this day our daily bread and forgive us our trespasses as we forgive those who trespass against us. And lead us not into temptation, but deliver us from the Evil One.

Open unto us the door of your loving kindness, O most blessed Mother of God. As we set our hope in you, let us not be confounded, but through you may we be delivered from all adversities. For you are the salvation of the Christian race.

---

[2] Lord Jesus Christ, Son of God, have mercy on me, the sinner.

The Wedding Feast at Cana

Ninth Decade

The Wedding at Cana

Let us remember-the miracle performed in Cana of Galilee when the Lord turned water into wine at the words of the Mother of God: *They have no wine.* Let us ask the Mother of God for help in our affairs and deliverance from need.

Rejoice, O Virgin, Mother of God, Mary, full of grace, the Lord is with you. Blessed are you among women and blessed is the fruit of your womb, for you have borne the Savior of our souls (Ten times).

After: Our Lady, Blessed Mother of God, help me in all my affairs and deliver me from every need and sorrow.

Our Father, Who are in heaven, hallowed be Your Name. Your kingdom come, Your will be done on earth as it is in heaven. Give us this day our daily bread and forgive us our trespasses as we forgive those who trespass against us. And lead us not into temptation, but deliver us from the Evil One.

Open unto us the door of your loving kindness, O most blessed Mother of God. As we set our hope in you, let us not be confounded, but through you may we be delivered from all adversities. For you are the salvation of the Christian race.

The Crucifixion of the Lord

Tenth Decade

The Crucifixion of the Lord

Let us remember the Mother of God standing at the Cross of the Lord, when grief pierced through her heart like a sword. Let us pray to the Mother of God for the strengthening of our souls and the banishment of despondency.

Rejoice, O Virgin, Mother of God, Mary, full of grace, the Lord is with you. Blessed are you among women and blessed is the fruit of your womb, for you have borne the Savior of our souls (Ten times).

After: Our Lady, Blessed Mother of God, strengthen my soul and banish my despair.

Our Father, Who are in heaven, hallowed be Your Name. Your kingdom come, Your will be done on earth as it is in heaven. Give us this day our daily bread and forgive us our trespasses as we forgive those who trespass against us. And lead us not into temptation, but deliver us from the Evil One.

Open unto us the door of your loving kindness, O most blessed Mother of God. As we set our hope in you, let us not be confounded, but through you may we be delivered from all adversities. For you are the salvation of the Christian race.

The Resurrection of Christ

Eleventh Decade

The Resurrection of the Lord

Let us remember the Resurrection of Christ and ask the Mother of God in prayer to resurrect our souls and give us new courage for spiritual feats.

Rejoice, O Virgin, Mother of God, Mary, full of grace, the Lord is with you. Blessed are you among women and blessed is the fruit of your womb, for you have borne the Savior of our souls (Ten times).

After: Our Lady, Blessed Mother of God, resurrect my soul and give me constant readiness for spiritual feats.

Our Father, Who are in heaven, hallowed be Your Name. Your kingdom come, Your will be done on earth as it is in heaven. Give us this day our daily bread and forgive us our trespasses as we forgive those who trespass against us. And lead us not into temptation, but deliver us from the Evil One.

Open unto us the door of your loving kindness, O most blessed Mother of God. As we set our hope in you, let us not be confounded, but through you may we be delivered from all adversities. For you are the salvation of the Christian race.

The Ascension of the Lord

Twelfth Decade

The Ascension of the Lord into Heaven

Let us remember the Ascension of Christ at which the Mother of God was present. Let us pray and ask the Queen of Heaven to raise up our souls from earthly and worldly amusements, and direct them to striving for higher things.

Rejoice, O Virgin, Mother of God, Mary, full of grace, the Lord is with you. Blessed are you among women and blessed is the fruit of your womb, for you have borne the Savior of our souls (Ten times).

After: Our Lady, Blessed Mother of God, deliver me from worldly thoughts and give me a mind and heart striving towards the salvation of my soul.

Our Father, Who are in heaven, hallowed be Your Name. Your kingdom come, Your will be done on earth as it is in heaven. Give us this day our daily bread and forgive us our trespasses as we forgive those who trespass against us. And lead us not into temptation, but deliver us from the Evil One.

Open unto us the door of your loving kindness, O most blessed Mother of God. As we set our hope in you, let us not be confounded, but through you may we be delivered from all adversities. For you are the salvation of the Christian race.

Pentecost

Thirteenth Decade

Pentecost

Let us remember the Upper Room and the descent of the Holy Spirit on the Apostles and the Mother of God. Let us pray:

> *Create in me a clean heart, O God; and renew a right spirit within me. Cast me not away from thy presence; and take not thy holy spirit from me* (Ps 51).

Rejoice, O Virgin, Mother of God, Mary, full of grace, the Lord is with you. Blessed are you among women and blessed is the fruit of your womb, for you have borne the Savior of our souls (Ten times).

After: Our Lady, Blessed Mother of God, make me a clean temple in which God's Holy Spirit will ever dwell.

Our Father, Who are in heaven, hallowed be Your Name. Your kingdom come, Your will be done on earth as it is in heaven. Give us this day our daily bread and forgive us our trespasses as we forgive those who trespass against us. And lead us not into temptation, but deliver us from the Evil One.

Open unto us the door of your loving kindness, O most blessed Mother of God. As we set our hope in you, let us not be confounded, but through you may we be delivered from all adversities. For you are the salvation of the Christian race.

The Dormition of the Theotokos

Fourteenth Decade

Dormition of the Theotokos

Let us remember the Dormition of the Blessed Mother of God and ask for a peaceful and serene end.

Rejoice, O Virgin, Mother of God, Mary, full of grace, the Lord is with you. Blessed are you among women and blessed is the fruit of your womb, for you have borne the Savior of our souls (Ten times).

After: Our Lady, Blessed Mother of God, grant me a peaceful and serene end.

Our Father, Who are in heaven, hallowed be Your Name. Your kingdom come, Your will be done on earth as it is in heaven. Give us this day our daily bread and forgive us our trespasses as we forgive those who trespass against us. And lead us not into temptation, but deliver us from the Evil One.

Open unto us the door of your loving kindness, O most blessed Mother of God. As we set our hope in you, let us not be confounded, but through you may we be delivered from all adversities. For you are the salvation of the Christian race.

The Theotokos, Queen of Heaven

FIFTEENTH DECADE

CROWNING OF THE THEOTOKOS BY THE HOLY TRINITY

Let us remember the glory of the Mother of God, with which the Lord crowned her after her removal from earth to heaven. Let us pray to the Queen of Heaven not to abandon the faithful who are on earth, but to defend them from every evil, covering them with her 41onourable and protecting veil.

Rejoice, O Virgin, Mother of God, Mary, full of grace, the Lord is with you. Blessed are you among women and blessed is the fruit of your womb, for you have borne the Savior of our souls (Ten times).

After: Our Lady, Blessed Mother of God, preserve me from every evil and cover me with your 41onourable protecting veil.

Our Father, Who are in heaven, hallowed be Your Name. Your kingdom come, Your will be done on earth as it is in heaven. Give us this day our daily bread and forgive us our trespasses as we forgive those who trespass against us. And lead us not into temptation, but deliver us from the Evil One.

Open unto us the door of your loving kindness, O most blessed Mother of God. As we set our hope in you, let us not be confounded, but through you may we be delivered from all adversities. For you are the salvation of the Christian race.

Final Prayers

It is truly meet to bless you, O Theotokos, ever blessed and most pure, and the Mother of God. More honourable than the Cherubim and beyond compare, more glorious than the Seraphim, who without corruption gave birth to God the Word, the very Theotokos, you do we magnify.

Glory to the Father, and to the Son, and to the Holy Spirit, both now and ever and unto the ages of ages. Amen.

Lord, have mercy (*Three times*).

O Lord, Jesus Christ, Son of God, for the sake of the prayers of Your most pure Mother, our holy and God-bearing fathers, and all the saints, have mercy on us. Amen.

RELICS OF THE THEOTOKOS

Ex capillis, Ex velo, Ex veste, Ex sepulchro
Beata Virgine Mariae

Overleaf are shown four precious relics of the Theotokos in a large Baroque, gilded, hand-carved and handmade reliquary. The relics consist of a short strand of hair (*ex capillis*) of the Virgin Mother of God, small pieces of her silk veil (*ex velo*) and colored robe (*ex veste*), and a stone from the tomb of her Dormition (*ex sepulchro*). According to tradition, the Virgin was wearing this silk veil when she gave birth to the Lord, Jesus Christ. The locks of hair, robe, and veil of the Theotokos were originally kept by the Patriarchs of Jerusalem, until the Patriarch-Saint Juvenal gave them to the Empress-Saint Pulcheria, who gifted them in turn to the city of Constantinople.

Locks from the hair of the Theotokos can now be found in the Great Reliquary, which is kept at the Duomo di Messina, Sicily. The silk veil of the Virgin was in the possession of the Emperor Charlemagne who received it as a gift from the Byzantine Empress Irene of Constantinople. It was gifted by Charlemagne's grandson, Charles II, to the Cathédrale Notre-Dame de Chartres, Chartres, France in 876. Other portions of the veil can now be found in churches across Italy, in Cologne and Mainz, Germany; and in Prague, Czech Republic among others. The tomb of the Dormition can be found in the crypt of the Church of the Assumption, Kidron Valley (valley of Josaphat), Jerusalem.

The authenticity of these relics of the Theotokos was certified in the 19th century by Aloysius, Cardinal Amat; head of the Roman Catholic College of Cardinals at the time. Detailed photographs of the relics can be seen on the next page.

Detail of the strand of hair (left) and small piece of the silk veil (right)

Detail of a small piece of the robe (left) and stone from the tomb (right)

Ex fascia, Beata Virgine Mariae

Small piece from the belt of the Theotokos, which according to tradition she gave to the Apostle Thomas. Large portions of the belt can now be found at Vatopedi Monastery, Mount Athos, Greece; at the Monastery of Trier, Germany, and in Georgia.

List of Icons

1.	Saint Seraphim of Sarov	Page 6
2.	The Birth of the Theotokos	12
3.	The Entrance of the Theotokos in the Temple	14
4.	The Annunciation of the Lord's Birth by the Archangel Gabriel	16
5.	The Visitation of the Theotokos with Righteous Elizabeth	18
6.	The Nativity of the Lord, Jesus Christ	20
7.	The Presentation of the Lord in the Temple	22
8.	The Flight into Egypt	24
9.	The Young Christ Teaching the Doctors in the Temple	26
10.	The Wedding Feast at Cana	28
11.	The Crucifixion of the Lord	30
12.	The Resurrection of Christ	32
13.	The Ascension of the Lord	34
14.	Pentecost	36
15.	The Dormition of the Theotokos	38
16.	The Theotokos, Queen of Heaven	40

List of Relics

1. *Ex capillis*   Pages 43, 45
2. *Ex velo*
3. *Ex veste*
4. *Ex sepulchro*
5. *Ex fascia*   Page 46

SELECT HOPE AND LIFE PRESS BOOKS

PURSUING HOLINESS
IN TODAY'S WORLD
ANGELO STAGNARO, OSF

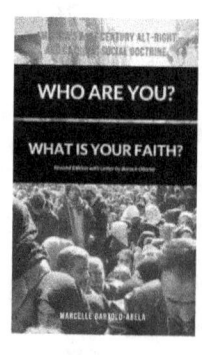

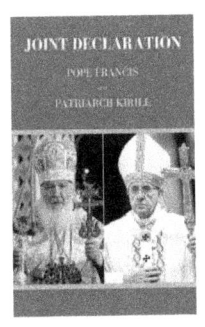

www.ingramcontent.com/pod-product-compliance
Lightning Source LLC
Chambersburg PA
CBHW050449010526
44118CB00013B/1744